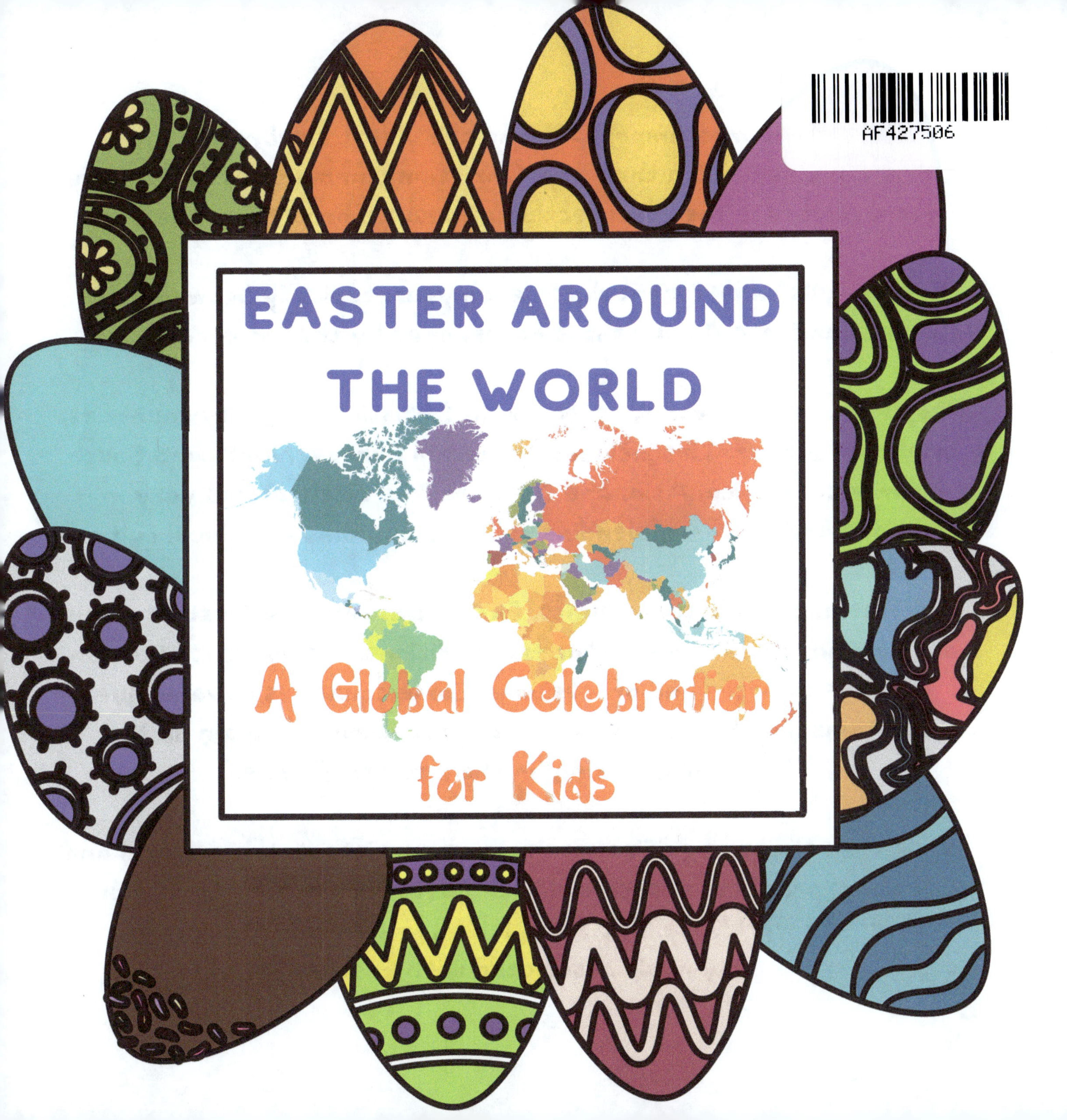
AF427506
EASTER AROUND THE WORLD
A Global Celebration for Kids

Easter is the most important and the oldest celebration in the Christian Church. On that day, Christian communities around the world celebrate the resurrection of Jesus Christ from the dead.

Easter falls on different dates each year, typically between late March and late April, as it is determined by the lunar calendar.

People around the world, especially in Christian-majority countries, celebrate Easter. This includes regions in Europe, North and South America, Africa, Asia, and Oceania. The celebrations vary in traditions and customs, blending religious customs with local culture.

In Western countries, egg hunts, Easter baskets, and festive meals are common. In Eastern Orthodox traditions, the focus is often on religious services and processions. Some countries have unique customs, like the "Semana Santa" processions in Spain or the "Paschal Greeting" in the Eastern Europe.

While the religious significance remains consistent, the cultural and regional practices associated with Easter contribute to its rich diversity worldwide. But first, let's see some mostly common symbols associated with Easter.

Easter Eggs: Decorated eggs are an universal symbol of Easter. In many cultures, they represent fertility and new life. Egg rolling, egg hunts, and egg decorating are common Easter activities.

Easter Bunny: The Easter Bunny is a beloved symbol, especially in Western countries. It is a symbol of fertility and is said to bring Easter eggs to children.

Lamb: The lamb is a symbol of Jesus, often referred to as the "Lamb of God" in Christian theology. Lamb dishes are common in Easter feasts.

Cross: The cross is a central symbol in Christianity, representing the crucifixion and resurrection of Jesus. Many churches use crosses as part of their Easter festivities.

Lilies: Lilies are often associated with Easter, symbolizing purity and the resurrection.

Hot Cross Buns: These spiced buns with a cross on top are traditional Easter treats in some cultures.

But each culture also added its unique stories, traditions and customs to the holidays. Thus, the Easter festivities are diverse and colorful across the globe.

Let's discover what makes Easter special in:

4

The adoption of Easter in Europe has deep historical roots and is closely tied to the spread of Christianity. The celebration of Easter dates back to the early days of Christianity when it became intertwined with existing pagan spring festivals. The Council of Nicaea in 325 AD established the date of Easter as the first Sunday following the first full moon after the vernal equinox, aligning it with both the Jewish Passover and the arrival of spring.

Alongside various church services, including Good Friday, Holy Saturday, and Easter Sunday., many European countries have developed unique cultural traditions associated with Easter. One widespread tradition is the decoration of eggs, symbolizing fertility and new life. This includes the painting, dyeing, and ornamentation of eggs, and some regions engage in egg-rolling competitions or other festive games

The Easter Bunny, a character associated with bringing eggs and gifts to children, is another popular European tradition, particularly in Germanic cultures. Children anticipate the Easter Bunny's visit, similar to the anticipation of Santa Claus during Christmas.

United Kingdom

Easter in the United Kingdom is a time of joyous celebration with a blend of religious customs, festive traditions, and delicious culinary delights. One iconic symbol is the Hot Cross Bun, a spiced sweet bun marked with a cross, traditionally eaten on Good friday. These buns are often enjoyed toasted with butter.

Easter Sunday brings the customary roast lamb dinner to many British households, symbolizing the spring season and renewal. Simnel Cake, a fruitcake with marzipan, is a cherished dessert, adorned with eleven marzipan balls representing the apostles (excluding Judas).

Children eagerly anticipate the Easter Egg Hunt, where colorful chocolate eggs are hidden in gardens or parks. Decorating eggs is a popular prelude to the hunt. In some regions, egg rolling competitions take place, with decorated hard-boiled eggs rolled down hills.

Easter bonnets are another delightful tradition, where children create and wear colorful hats adorned with flowers, ribbons, and decorations. Many participate in Easter parades showcasing their festive bonnets.

Church services are integral to Easter observances, particularly the Easter Vigil and Easter Sunday services, where the resurrection of Jesus is celebrated. Many towns host parades and community events, adding a festive atmosphere to the holiday.

In different regions of the UK, there are unique traditions like "pace egging" in Lancashire, where decorated eggs are exchanged for coins. Morris dancing, a traditional English folk dance, is also performed in some areas during Easter festivities.

8

GERMANY

In Germany, on Easter, trees are adorned with colorful eggs, both real and decorative, much like Christmas trees. Decorating eggs is a cherished tradition, with intricate designs and vibrant colors.

Easter Sunday brings a festive feast, and roast lamb or ham is a common centerpiece. "Osterlamm" or Easter lamb cake, is a popular dessert shaped like a lamb, symbolizing innocence and the Lamb of God in Christian tradition.

Children eagerly await the Easter Egg Hunt, or "Eiersuche," where eggs are hidden in gardens or parks. The eggs may be filled with chocolates, candies, or small toys. Actually, the Easter Bunny tradition originated in Germany. Egg rolling competitions are also held, with decorated eggs rolled down hills to symbolize the rolling away of the stone from Jesus's tomb.

Easter bonfires, known as "Osterfeuer," are lit on Easter Saturday in some regions, symbolizing the triumph of light over darkness. Attendees gather around the bonfires for socializing and festivities.

Religious services, particularly the Easter Vigil and Easter Sunday services, play a significant role in German Easter celebrations. Many towns also host processions, including the traditional "Ostermarsch," a march celebrating the arrival of spring.

GREECE

The Greek Orthodox Church plays a central role in the festivities, with Holy Week, known as "Megali Evdomada," leading up to Easter Sunday being a period of intense religious observance.

On Good Friday, the epitaphios (a decorated bier symbolizing the burial of Christ) is carried through the streets in a solemn procession, accompanied by mournful hymns. On Holy Saturday night, the Resurrection service takes place, marked by the midnight "Anastasi" ceremony, where the resurrection of Christ is celebrated with an incredible number of lit candles and the joyful exclamation "Christos Anesti" (Christ is Risen).

A unique Easter tradition in Greece is the cracking of decorated eggs. Family and friends engage in a game of egg tapping, where each person holds a red egg and takes turns trying to crack the eggs of others. The last remaining uncracked egg is believed to bring good luck.

Easter Sunday is a day of feasting, with lamb being the centerpiece of the celebratory meal. Spit-roasted lamb, known as "Arni sto souvla," is a popular dish, and families often gather for festive meals that include a variety of traditional Greek delicacies.

Children actively participate in the festivities, joining in the egg-cracking game and enjoying special Easter treats. It's common for children to receive small gifts and sweets during the celebrations.

 ITALY

Italy's diverse regions contribute their variations, from the religious fervor of Sicily to the historic charm of Venice. Each locale weaves its distinctive thread into the rich fabric of Italian Easter, uniting communities in shared traditions of faith, food, and familial warmth.

In Rome, the heart of Catholicism, Easter unfolds with grandiosity as the Pope delivers the "Urbi et Orbi" blessing from St. Peter's Basilica. The city's ancient streets become a stage for processions and religious fervor, creating a palpable atmosphere of reverence.

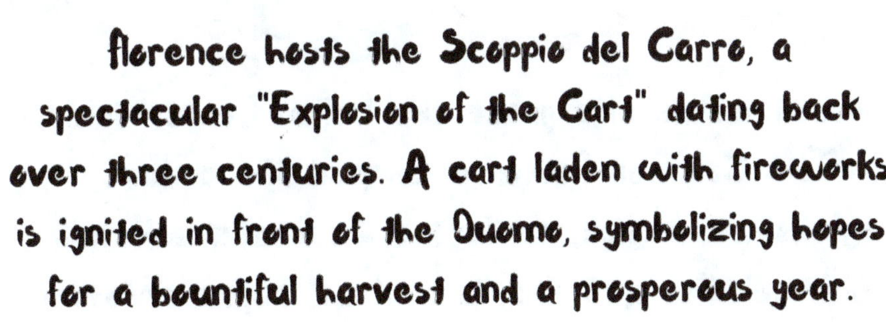

Florence hosts the Scoppio del Carro, a spectacular "Explosion of the Cart" dating back over three centuries. A cart laden with fireworks is ignited in front of the Duomo, symbolizing hopes for a bountiful harvest and a prosperous year.

In some regions, cheese rolling replaces the egg rolling other countries are so used to.

Italian Easter tables boast a centerpiece of roasted lamb, a symbolic dish representing sacrifice and renewal. "Agnello al forno" is a culinary tradition enjoyed during Easter lunch, adding savory richness to the festive feast.

Easter Monday, or "La Pasquetta," extends the celebration with a uniquely Italian twist. Families often escape to the countryside for picnics, reveling in the beauty of nature and creating lasting memories.

Sweet treats also grace the Italian Easter table. The Colomba Pasquale, shaped like a dove, symbolizes peace, while the Scarcella, adorned with colorful sprinkles, is a visual representation of abundance and joy. Huge chocolate eggs are another popular treat.

POLAND

Holy Week in Poland is marked by solemn processions, especially on Good friday, when people participate in the "Way of the Cross" to commemorate the Passion of Christ. Churches are adorned with symbolic tree branches and flowers.

On Holy Saturday, the blessing of Easter baskets, known as "Swieconka," is a cherished tradition. families bring baskets filled with a variety of symbolic foods like bread, eggs, and sausage to be blessed by the priest.

Easter Sunday's centerpiece dish is "Biała Kiełbasa," a traditional white sausage, often enjoyed alongside hard-boiled eggs, horseradish, and a special Easter bread called "Babka."

Poles love their Easter sweets, especially the famous "Mazurek" cake.

Easter Monday also involves "Smigus-Dyngus," a water-throwing tradition where children and adults playfully splash water on one another. This joyful activity symbolizes cleansing of sins and renewal, reflecting the spirit of Easter.

Polish Easter eggs, or "Pisanki," are intricately decorated with vibrant colors and traditional patterns. Children often engage in egg decorating activities, creating beautiful and symbolic artworks to share with family and friends.

HUNGARY

Holy Week is observed with solemnity in Hungary, featuring church services and processions, especially on Good Friday, when people reflect on the crucifixion of Jesus.

On Easter Sunday families gather for a festive meal, sharing the joy of Easter together. The centerpiece is a special dish called "Sonka Tojassal," which consists of ham and eggs. Traditional Hungarian Easter sweets, such as the "Kalacs" (sweet bread) and "Turos Csusza" (noodle dish with cottage cheese), add a delightful touch to the Easter table.

Children actively participate in Easter egg decorating, creating vibrant and artistic designs on eggs, a tradition known as "Husveti Tojasfestes." These decorated eggs are often exchanged among friends and family.

One distinctive Hungarian tradition is the "Sprinkling Monday". Boys playfully sprinkle perfumed water on girls on Easter Monday, symbolizing fertility and the arrival of spring. Boys visit girls home, recite poems, sprinkle them with perfume and receive treats. It's a day of joy and surprises.

In addition to the playful water sprinkling, children often participate in egg rolling competitions, where eggs are rolled down hills.

Throughout Hungary, regional variations may introduce additional customs, but the common thread is the emphasis on family, shared meals, and the joyous celebration of Easter. It's a time when Hungarians come together to observe traditions, savor delicious dishes, and celebrate the renewal of life and faith.

SPAIN

Easter in Spain, known as Semana Santa, is a deeply religious and culturally rich celebration. It begins with solemn processions, especially in cities like Seville and Granada, where elaborately decorated floats depicting biblical scenes are carried through the streets. In some regions, effigies of Judas are burned on Easter Sunday.

One distinctive tradition is the "Paso," which involves religious statues carried by "costaleros," or float-bearers, showcasing scenes from the Passion of Christ. Children play a significant role in Semana Santa, participating in processions as "Nazarenos," wearing traditional hooded robes. They often take part in reenactments of the Stations of the Cross.

Easter Sunday, or "Domingo de Resurreccion," marks the joyous culmination of Semana Santa. families come together for festive meals, featuring dishes like "Cordero Lechal" (suckling lamb) or "Potaje de Vigilia," a hearty lentil and codfish stew, taking center stage. Traditional sweets like "Torrijas," sweet fried bread soaked in milk and honey, and "Mona de Pascua," a sweet Easter cake, are enjoyed during this time.

In some regions, children engage in the tradition of "Monas de Pascua," decorating Easter eggs and creating colorful chocolate figures. These festive treats are often given as gifts.

Throughout Spain, regional variations add unique flavors to the celebrations. Whether it's the somber processions in Andalusia or the vibrant festivities in Catalonia, Easter in Spain is a time when communities unite to express faith, savor traditional dishes, and embrace the cultural richness of Semana Santa.

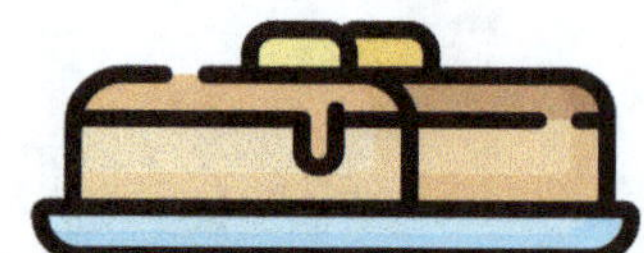

 FINLAND

The finnish Easter combines both religious and pagan elements. families often attend church services to mark the religious significance of the holiday.

Virpominen is a unique Easter tradition where children dress up as Easter witches, carry decorated willow branches, and visit homes to exchange blessings or drawinings for sweets. This charming custom combines folklore with the joy of Easter.

Easter Saturday is a day for outdoor activities, with many families heading to their cottages or spending time in nature to embrace the arrival of spring.

The "Munajahti," or Easter egg hunt, is a beloved activity for finnish children. They eagerly search for chocolate eggs hidden around homes and gardens, adding an element of fun and excitement to the holiday.

Bonfires are lit in some regions, where people gather to celebrate and, according to tradition, ward off witches and evil spirits.

Traditional Easter dishes in finland often include lamb, salmon, pickled herring and the iconic "Mammi." Mammi is a dark, sweet malt pudding served with cream and sugar, a distinctive and acquired taste enjoyed during the holiday. finnish Easter often includes visits to "Mammi buffets," where they can experience this traditional treat in different forms.

Easter in finland is a time for families to come together, celebrate unique traditions, savor delicious food, and embrace the beauty of spring.

NORWAY

In Norway, the emphasis is on family unity, delicious food, and the observance of Easter traditions that reflect the country's rich cultural heritage.

One distinct Norwegian Easter tradition is the "Paskekrim," or Easter crime. Many Norwegians indulge in crime novels and detective shows during the Easter holiday, making it a popular time for mystery-themed entertainment.

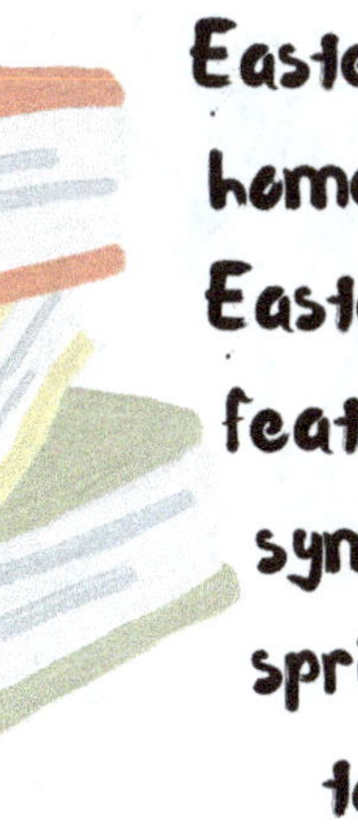

Easter decorations brighten homes with vibrant colors. Easter twigs adorned with feathers and painted eggs symbolize the arrival of spring and add a festive touch to households.

Easter Saturday is a time for family gatherings and festive meals. Norwegian Easter dishes often feature lamb, a symbol of spring and renewal. Many Norwegians partake in the customary Easter lamb roast, to celebrate the season. "Pinnekjott," a dish of dried and salted lamb ribs, is a traditional favorite, especially in Western Norway.

Children actively participate in joyous Easter egg hunts, eagerly searching for colorful eggs filled with candies or small toys.

Easter Sunday's often involves a special family meal, with various traditional dishes such as "Rakfisk" (fermented fish) or "Lutefisk" (dried fish treated with lye) in certain regions.

Easter Monday is a time for outdoor activities. families often engage in excursions, hikes, or skiing, enjoying the emerging spring landscapes.

ROMANIA

Easter traditions and dishes in Romania vary a lot by region, depending on who influenced the area the most, the Austro-Hungarians, the Russians or the Turks.

Easter Saturday, or "Sambata Mare," is marked by the midnight church service, where the Resurrection is celebrated with joyous processions and the sharing of the Holy Light from one person to another.

Easter eggs play a significant role, with intricate designs adorning eggs in vibrant colors. These eggs are often exchanged as gifts and symbolize rebirth and renewal.

In the eastern part of the country, on Saturday evening, people leave a red egg and a coin in a bowl of water that they use on Saturday morning to wash their faces. It's believed that this way they will be healthy and lucky.

Easter Sunday, or "Duminica Pastelui," is a day for family gatherings and festive meals. Easter dishes in Romania include lamb meat and "Drob de Miel," a lamb organs based dish. Lamb represents sacrifice and renewal. As per desserts, "cozonac", a rolled dough with nuts and cocoa, and "pasca", a cheese cake, are the most common.

One tradition that can be observed throughout the country is Easter egg cracking. In this Easter game, participants compete to see whose decorated egg remains uncracked the longest. Children and adults gather around the table, try to spot the luckiest egg, grab it and attempt to crack the opponent's egg while keeping their own intact. The winner is the one that still has the egg uncracked at the end of the game.

Throughout Romania, regional variations may add unique elements to the celebrations, but the overarching theme revolves around the joy of spring, family togetherness, and the observance of Easter traditions that reflect the country's rich cultural heritage.

 FRANCE

Easter in france is a time of joyous celebrations. The french celebrate Easter for religious reasons, but also to welcome spring and create moments of happiness with family and friends.

One charming tradition is the "cloches volantes" or flying bells. Church bells are silent from Good friday until Easter Sunday morning, symbolizing mourning and resurrection. Legend has it that on Easter Sunday, church bells fly to the Vatican and return with chocolate treats. It's like a magical journey of sweets and surprises.

Easter eggs, or "Oeufs de Paques," are a focal point of the celebration. These eggs are beautifully decorated and often filled with chocolates or small toys. The tradition of egg hunts, or "Chasse aux oeufs," is a beloved activity for children.

Easter Sunday, or "Dimanche de Paques" starts with a special church service, and families gather for festive meals. Lamb dishes, representing the sacrificial lamb of Easter, are commonly enjoyed.

In the Provence region, there's a unique tradition called the "Giant Omelette of Bessieres." Locals come together to prepare a massive omelette using thousands of eggs to symbolize abundance and community.

Easter Monday, or "Lundi de Paques," is often a day for outdoor activities. families may take walks or enjoy picnics, celebrating the arrival of spring.

The "Colombes de Paques," or Easter doves, are sweet pastries shaped like doves, symbolizing peace and renewal. They are commonly enjoyed during Easter in various regions of france.

28

ESTONIA

Estonians celebrate Easter to welcome spring and create moments of happiness with family and friends. Many decorate birch twigs with colorful ribbons and place them on doorsteps or exchange them for treats. This symbolizes the welcoming of spring and is believed to bring good luck.

Easter Sunday typically begins with a visit to the church for a special service, marking the Resurrection of Christ. Families then gather for a festive meal. Traditional Estonian Easter dishes include smoked ham, braided sweet bread, "Pashka," a sweet cheese dessert, and various lamb dishes. Eggs are dyed and used in a variety of Easter recipes, contributing to the festive table.

Easter Monday is a public holiday in Estonia. Families often engage in outdoor activities, picnics, or visits to parks to enjoy the emerging spring landscape. Kids engage in eggs roll competitions, symbol of the rolling away of the stone from Jesus' tomb.

The "Easter Swing," or "Kiiking," is a traditional Estonian activity where individuals swing on a large swing, attempting to go over the crossbar. This is a symbolic gesture of swinging away the winter and embracing the coming spring

Children are actively involved in the tradition of "Easter egg rolling." Decorated eggs are rolled down slopes, and the unbroken ones are considered a symbol of good luck and prosperity.

The "Easter Bunny" tradition has also found its way into Estonian celebrations. Children anticipate the Easter Bunny's visit, and egg hunts are organized, adding an element of excitement to the festivities.

LUXEMBOURG

One distinct Luxembourgish Easter tradition is the "Eimaischen," a lively market held on Easter Monday in Luxembourg City's Grund district. Artisans showcase and sell traditional pottery, crafts, and decorated eggs.

Easter Sunday, or "Paques," often starts with a visit to church, followed by a festive family meal. Lamb dishes, symbolizing spring and renewal, are commonly featured on the Easter menu.

The "Easter Egg Hunt" tradition is cherished by Luxembourgish children. Decorated eggs, chocolate treats, and small toys are hidden, and children eagerly search for them in gardens and homes.

The "Peckvillercher" tradition involves crafting small figurines out of bread dough. These whimsical characters, shaped like birds, are baked and exchanged as tokens of goodwill among friends and family.

Easter Monday, or "Ouschtermeindeg," is a public holiday in Luxembourg. families often spend the day outdoors, enjoying picnics or taking part in community events.

"Hechesblein," or Easter Monday games, are organized in some regions. Traditional games include egg rolling and egg throwing contests, adding a playful element to the holiday.

MALTA

Easter in Malta is a festive and deeply religious celebration. Public processions, featuring statues of the Risen Christ, the Virgin Mary, and other religious figures, are a common sight in towns and villages. These processions create a solemn yet celebratory atmosphere.

The "Rabat Good friday Procession" is a significant event, known for its poignant reenactment of the Passion of Christ. It involves the participation of both adults and children, creating a powerful visual representation of the Easter story.

Easter Sunday is marked by a festive meal that includes traditional Maltese dishes. Roast lamb, baked pasta, and "Kwarezimal," a type of Lenten sweet, are commonly enjoyed. One distinctive Maltese Easter tradition is the "figolla", a special Easter pastry made of almond paste, often shaped into symbolic figures like lambs, crosses, or hearts, and decorated with icing.

Easter Monday, or "It-Tnejn tax-Xellug," is a public holiday in Malta. Families often engage in outdoor activities, picnics, or visit historical sites, enjoying the spring weather.

Children actively participate in the "Easter egg hunts" searching for hidden eggs in gardens and homes. The eggs are often beautifully decorated and filled with chocolates or small toys.

The "Cirkeb" is a traditional Maltese game where children use painted wooden balls to hit each other's "Cirkeb" in an open field, adding a playful and cultural element to the Easter celebrations.

34

South America adopted Easter through the influence of Spanish and Portuguese colonization, bringing Catholicism to the region.

Over the centuries, South American countries have integrated their own cultural elements into Easter celebrations, adding unique touches to the observance of this religious holiday.

For instance, in some areas, communities organize reenactments of the Last Supper, washing the feet of the poor, or other rituals that emphasize humility and service.

BRASIL

Easter in Brazil is a vibrant and culturally rich celebration that combines religious traditions with samba rhythms and lively festivities.

The country, with its predominantly Catholic population, marks Holy Week with processions, church services, and reenactments of Jesus' crucifixion and resurrection. Brazilian cities like Ouro Preto are renowned for elaborate Semana Santa events

Local customs include the "Queima de Judas," burning effigies of Judas Iscariot, symbolizing betrayal, but also the triumph of good over evil.

A popular tradition is the "Easter Egg Battle."
families gather for egg-cracking competitions,
where the owner of the last uncracked egg is
considered the winner.

On Easter Monday, families and communities come together for music, dance,
and joyous gatherings, creating memories filled with laughter and
togetherness. It's like a big, happy carnival, celebrating life and the spirit of
Easter.

Culinary delights include feijoada (black bean stew), tasty codfish dishes and
the traditional "pacoca" bread, enjoyed during this festive time.

COLOMBIA

Easter in Colombia is a vibrant blend of religious fervor and cultural celebrations. Semana Santa (Holy Week) is a significant time marked by processions, elaborate street displays, and solemn religious rituals. Throughout the country, particularly in cities like Popayan, Mompox, and Zipaquira, communities engage in traditional reenactments of Jesus' journey to the cross.

Colombians participate in processions carrying statues and religious images, emphasizing the religious significance of Easter. Intricate sawdust carpets (alfombras) line the streets, showcasing vibrant designs and religious symbols. The "Viacrucis" or Stations of the Cross is a common practice, with believers reenacting the biblical events.

Children and adults in Colombia add artistic touches to the celebration, creating vibrant sawdust carpets ("alfombras") or crafting intricate palm frond decorations, like palm crosses. They symbolize blessings and protection, turning a simple palm frond into an expression of faith.

Colombian cuisine also plays a role, with traditional dishes like "fanesca" and "empanadas" enjoyed during this period. Tamales and tasty fish dishes are also enjoyed.

PERU

Easter in Peru is a captivating blend of ancient traditions and fervent religious celebrations. Semana Santa unfolds with rich cultural displays and deep spiritual significance. In cities like Ayacucho, elaborate processions feature meticulously crafted religious statues paraded through the streets.

Distinctive to Peru is the traditional "Dance of the Scissors" (Danza de las Tijeras), where skilled performers engage in intricate dances using large scissors, symbolizing the triumph of life over death. The city of Cusco showcases the "Lord of the Earthquakes" procession, a unique blend of Inca and Catholic traditions.

Communities participate in the creation of stunning street art with vibrant carpets made of colored sawdust and flowers. In some regions, the "Toritos de Pucara", bull-shaped structures adorned with colorful decorations, are paraded, symbolizing protection and fertility.

Peruvian cuisine also takes center stage with special Easter dishes like "fanescas", a traditional soup enjoyed during this period.

NORTH AMERICA

Easter was adopted in North America through the arrival of European settlers, primarily from England and other European countries with Christian traditions. The celebration of Easter in North America shares common roots with European Easter traditions, but it has also evolved over the centuries with cultural influences and regional variations.

The Easter Bunny, for example, is a cultural symbol that likely has its origins in German folklore but became popularized in the United States in the 18th century.

In the **USA**, Easter is a joyful time filled with colorful eggs, sweet treats, and family celebrations. People celebrate the holiday to remember Jesus and welcome spring.

One of the most iconic Easter traditions is the annual Easter Monday Egg Roll at the White House. Happy children race colorful eggs trying to get them as far as possible without breaking them. But, in order to do this, they have to be lucky first. Each year there is a free lottery organized. The winners and some select guests get to roll their eggs on the green lawn at the White House.

However, there are other customs in which everyone can take part. Easter egg decorating and Easter eggs hunts are popular throughout the states. Children look forward to these funny competitions in which they search for hidden eggs filled with candies or small toys.

On Easter morning, children wake up excited to find baskets filled with goodies from the Easter Bunny. It's a tradition for kids to leave carrots for the bunny the night before.

Some cities also organize parades with festive floats and people dressed in Easter-themed costumes.

Traditional foods include hot cross buns, a sweet bread marked with a cross.

44

for Canadians, Easter is a mix of religious traditions and festive activities. families often attend church services on both Good friday and Easter Sunday to reflect on the importance of Easter in the Christian faith.

Children eagerly anticipate the Easter Bunny's visit. On Sunday mornig they find baskets filled with chocolates, candies and small toys. It's a magical moment as they discover the surprises left by the Easter Bunny.

On Easter Sunday, families gather for a special meal. A popular dish is ham, and dessert often includes sweet treats like chocolate eggs and bunnies. Hot cross buns are also enjoyed.

Most families also engage in fun activities like hunting for decorated eggs in parks or gardens. Egg rolling is also very popular. Some communities organize parades with colorful floats and lively music.

In essence, Easter in Canada is a blend of joyful festivities and meaningful traditions. It's a time when families come together to celebrate, share delicious meals, and create lasting memories of happiness and togetherness.

46

MEXICO

In Mexico, the Holy Week, also known as Semana Santa is marked by elaborate Passion Plays, theatrical presentations that depict the events of Jesus' final days. These plays may be performed in town squares or even in the streets. Participants, often dressed in traditional robes, carry statues and reenact scenes from the Bible. Streets are often decorated with colorful sawdust carpets known as "alfombras" for processions to pass over.

Children in Mexico are like little artists before Easter. They engage in joyful activities like crafting vibrant papel picado decorations or creating colorful cascarones (decorated eggshells).

The midnight Mass, known as "La Misa de Gallo," is a key component of the Easter celebration. In some regions, the "Burning of Judas" is another symbolic ritual on Holy Saturday night. Effigies of Judas Iscariot, made of paper or other materials, are burned in public spaces to symbolize the betrayal of Jesus.

On Easter, mexicans enjoy a delicious meal with traditional foods — savory mole, tasty fish dishes, and sweet treats.

 BERMUDA ISLANDS

Bermuda is a self-governing British Overseas Territory in the Atlantic Ocean known for its pink-sand beaches. Being close to the Americas, the islands have adopted customs and traditions from both UK and the USA. But they also added their own spin to the celebrations, making Easter in Bermuda joyful and truly unique.

The days before Easter are full of excitement. families prepare by cleaning their homes and creating beautiful decorations.

On Good friday, children in Bermuda participate in delightful kite-flying competitions, turning the sky into a colorful display. The kites symbolize the ascent of Jesus after the Resurrection.

49

Another charming custom is the "Bermuda onion" tradition. families exchange onions, symbolizing renewal and the island's history. It's like a unique twist to Easter, celebrating local traditions with a touch of humor.

Easter Monday is an extra day of fun with the "Easter Parade." Locals dress in vibrant attire and stroll through the streets, showcasing Bermuda's colorful culture. The lively procession, spreads joy and showcases the island's spirit.

As per the food, Bermudians enjoy a flavorful Easter meal, with fish chowder, hot cross buns, and sweet treats.

In many Asian countries, the adoption of Easter is closely tied to the presence of Christian communities. Missionaries and European colonization played a great role in introducing Christian traditions, including Easter, to various parts of Asia.

As Christianity spread, local communities embraced and integrated Easter into their culture. However, its observance in Asia is often limited. While Easter shares universal Christian themes, the specific customs and traditions vary, showcasing the adaptability of the holiday in diverse cultural contexts.

In predominantly non-Christian countries, Easter may not be widely observed beyond Christian communities.

Easter in the Philippines is a beloved celebration marked by unique traditions.

Holy Week, starting with Palm Sunday, witnesses the blessing of palm fronds and processions depicting the Passion of Christ.

Good friday is a solemn day with filipinos engaging in various acts of penance, including reenactments and processions. However, the highlight of Easter is the "Salubong" or "Encounter" on Easter Sunday.

In the early hours of the morning, statues of the resurrected Christ and the Virgin Mary, adorned with flowers, are paraded through the streets. The climax of the celebration occurs when the two statues meet, symbolizing the reunion of Jesus and Mary. This event is accompanied by joyful singing, fireworks, and a palpable sense of community.

Another tradition is the "Easter Egg Kasaysayan". People create colorful eggs with historical themes, showcasing the rich filipino culture.

Children play a central role in the Easter festivities. Easter egg hunts are popular, with children enthusiastically searching for hidden eggs filled with treats. The joyous atmosphere extends to games, storytelling, and other activities designed for the younger members of the community.

As with many filipino celebrations, food is a crucial element of Easter. families gather for festive meals featuring special dishes like "lechon" (roast pig), "bibingka" (rice cake), and "suman" (sticky rice).

53

 INDIA

In India, the Easter festivities of the relatively small Christian community blend religious themes with local traditions. The festivities commence with Palm Sunday, marked by the blessing of palm leaves and processions, symbolizing Jesus' triumphant entry into Jerusalem.

Good friday is observed solemnly, with church services focusing on the Passion of Christ. In some regions, reenactments of the Stations of the Cross take place. However, the joyous culmination of Easter Sunday brings a sense of renewal and hope.

Indian Christian communities, like in Goa and Kerala, engage in vibrant celebrations. Special church services, including the Easter Vigil, are attended by families dressed in new clothes. The traditional lighting of the Paschal candle symbolizes the resurrection.

Children participate in decorating churches with vibrant flowers and creating colorful rangoli designs. Churches often organize Easter egg hunts, a popular activity borrowed from Western countries, creating a festive atmosphere for the younger members of the community.

Traditional Indian dishes are incorporated into Easter feasts. families prepare a variety of regional specialties, such as biryani, appam, and coconut-based curries. Sweets like "neurees" and "bebinca" add a sweet touch to the celebration.

 South Korea

In South Korea, Easter is celebrated by the Christian community, and while it's not as widely observed as in some other countries, there are unique traditions that make the occasion special.

Easter Sunday church services are the focal point of the celebration, featuring prayers, hymns, and sermons centered around the resurrection of Jesus Christ. families often attend these services together, dressed in their finest attire.

One unique tradition is the making and sharing of "bingeoppang," fish-shaped pastries filled with sweet red bean paste. These pastries are a popular street food during Easter, and families may also make them at home as a special treat.

Children are involved in various activities, including Easter egg hunts organized by churches or community groups. These hunts add an element of excitement for the younger members of the community. In some schools and communities, Easter-themed arts and crafts activities are organized.

While Easter in South Korea may not be as widely celebrated as other holidays, it provides an opportunity for the Christian community to come together, reflect on the significance of the resurrection, and enjoy shared traditions and treats that make the occasion memorable.

In Japan, Easter is not a widely celebrated religious holiday, as Christianity is a minority religion. However, there is a growing interest in the cultural aspects of Easter, and some unique traditions have emerged.

One popular Easter tradition in Japan is the custom of exchanging beautifully decorated eggs, similar to the Western practice of giving Easter eggs. These eggs may be intricately painted or adorned with colorful patterns.

Some families and communities organize "Hanami Egg Hunts" beneath cherry blossom trees, adding a unique twist to this western Easter tradition.

While Easter is not associated with a specific meal in Japan, families might take the opportunity to enjoy a special meal together. This could include a variety of Japanese dishes or seasonal desserts, like Sakura-flavored treats, or even international cuisine, reflecting the diverse culinary influences in the country.

In recent years, themed events and decorations in shopping malls and entertainment districts have become more prevalent during the Easter season. These events often feature Easter bunny characters, egg decorations, and interactive activities for children.

Easter in Japan is not a religious event for the majority but rather a cultural celebration that allows people to embrace the joyful and colorful aspects of the holiday. The focus is on creating a fun and festive atmosphere for families, and the unique blend of cultural elements adds a distinct flavor to the Japanese observance of Easter.

ISRAEL

In Israel, Easter holds significant religious importance, particularly in Jerusalem, where many Christian traditions originated. The celebration of Easter, known as "Pesach" in Hebrew, is a blend of both religious and cultural practices.

Easter Sunday is marked by special church services, with the Church of the Holy Sepulchre in Jerusalem being a focal point for Christian pilgrims. The Holy fire ceremony, a longstanding tradition, takes place on Holy Saturday, where a flame is believed to miraculously appear in the Church of the Holy Sepulchre and is then distributed to various churches in the world.

Children in Israel actively participate in Easter festivities, engaging in various activities such as decorating eggs. The eggs are often dyed in vibrant colors and symbolize new life and the resurrection.

Traditional dishes play a significant role in the Easter feast. "Ma'amoul," a sweet pastry filled with dates or nuts, is a popular treat during this time. Additionally, lamb dishes, symbolizing sacrifice, are often prepared as part of the festive meals.

Despite the diverse cultural and religious landscape in Israel, Easter is celebrated with respect for the Christian traditions, and the blend of ancient customs with contemporary practices creates a unique and vibrant atmosphere during this important holiday.

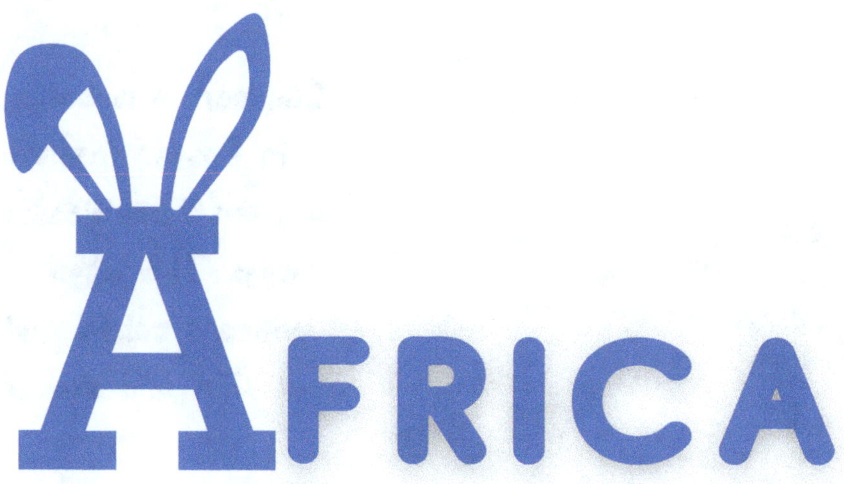AFRICA

Easter reached Africa through the spread of Christianity during colonial periods and missionary efforts. Today, many African countries celebrate Easter, marking the resurrection of Jesus Christ. Easter is embraced as a time of spiritual reflection, communal unity, and celebration.

Some countries have religious services, processions, and church activities similar to those in other parts of the world. But most of them add unique touches to the observance, incorporating local customs, art, music and cuisine into the festivities.

Easter symbols, such as eggs and rabbits, may be interpreted and incorporated into local African contexts, blending Christian symbolism with indigenous meanings.

Easter in Nigeria is a time of joy and celebration. Families gather for special church services and prayers. In some communities, there are lively processions and parades with music and dance.

Children often engage in Easter egg painting and egg hunts, searching for little treasures hidden in gardens.

In coastal regions, particularly Lagos, communities engage in vibrant processions to the beaches on Good Friday, symbolizing Jesus' journey to Golgotha. This unique custom is called "Eyo" festival. It combines religious observances with cultural expressions.

Easter Monday is a public holiday, and families go on outings, picnics, or enjoy outdoor games. It's a day dedicated to joy, laugther and bonding with the loved ones

Traditional Nigerian dishes, like jollof rice and fried chicken, are prepared for festive meals. Many people also wear colorful traditional attire called "aso ebi" to mark the occasion.

ETHIOPIA

Easter in Ethiopia, called Fasika, is a special celebration. The days before Easter, families prepare by cleaning their homes, attending church services, and lighting candles.

On Saturday evening, Ethiopians gather for a special ceremony that lasts all night, singing hymns and celebrating the resurrection. Everyone wears new clothes.

Children participate in processions, waving palm branches to remember Jesus' entry into Jerusalem..

A big feast is prepared, featuring injera (a flatbread) and doro wat (spicy chicken stew). Families share meals with friends and neighbors, showing kindness and love. In some places, there are horse races and games, adding excitement to the festivities.

Ethiopian children also enjoy the tradition of painting and decorating eggs, just like in other parts of the world. Fasika is a time for joy, prayers, and being together with loved ones, celebrating the hope and happiness of Easter

Easter in Kenya is a joyous occasion marked by vibrant celebrations and traditional customs. families attend special church services, where lively music and prayers fill the air.

In some communities, there are colorful processions and parades, with people wearing traditional attire, singing, and dancing. It's a time for unity and community spirit.

Children participate in Easter egg decorating and egg hunts, searching for small hidden surprises in gardens or parks.

A tradition Kenyans are very fond of is the preparation of special meals, featuring dishes like nyama choma (grilled meat) and chapati. families gather to share these delicious meals and enjoy each other's company.

Easter Monday is often a public holiday, allowing families to go on outings, picnics, or engage in outdoor games. Kenyan children eagerly look forward to receiving treats and small gifts during this festive time.

MOROCCO

Morocco, a predominantly Muslim country, doesn't have widespread Easter celebrations due to its Islamic traditions. However, during the spring season, families and communities engage in other cultural and local festivities.

People in Morocco cherish the arrival of spring, appreciating the changing landscapes and the beauty of nature. families often gather for special meals, and children partake in outdoor activities, enjoying the pleasant weather.

While Easter itself is not a focal point, the spirit of renewal and togetherness is celebrated in ways that align with the country's cultural values. Traditional music, dances, and communal events may take place, fostering a sense of community and joy during the spring season.

In Morocco, as in many Muslim-majority countries, the emphasis is on Islamic holidays, and Easter is not as widely observed. However, Morocco offers a welcoming and diverse environment where people come together to celebrate life and culture during the spring season.

AUSTRALIA

Easter typically falls during the autumn season in Australia, creating a unique atmosphere for the celebrations.

One notable Australian Easter tradition is the "Easter Bilby" campaign. Due to the conservation concerns surrounding the endangered bilby (a native marsupial) and the desire to raise awareness about wildlife conservation, chocolate bilbies have become an alternative to the traditional Easter bunny chocolate. This initiative encourages support for Australian wildlife and habitat preservation.

Children in Australia actively participate in Easter egg hunts, a popular and cherished tradition. Community events and local parks often organize these hunts, where children search for chocolate eggs hidden in gardens or designated areas. This activity brings joy and excitement to children as they embark on the Easter egg hunt adventure.

The Australian Easter celebration also includes festive meals with family and friends. As Easter coincides with the autumn harvest, traditional dishes often feature seasonal fruits and vegetables. Lamb, a popular meat choice, is commonly enjoyed during Easter feasts, symbolizing renewal and sacrifice.

Hot cross buns, spiced and sweetened buns marked with a cross on top, are a staple during Easter in Australia. These buns, often enjoyed toasted with butter, have become synonymous with the holiday and are available in bakeries and supermarkets leading up to Easter.

Australian families may take advantage of the long weekend by engaging in outdoor activities, such as camping, barbecues, or trips to the beach, making the most of the pleasant autumn weather.

CONCLUSIONS

And there you have it, friends! We've hopped around the globe, exploring Easter traditions that are as diverse as the colors in a springtime meadow.

From egg hunts in the United States to "Eimaischen" markets in Luxembourg, we've discovered how people everywhere celebrate this egg-citing holiday. It's like a global Easter egg hunt, but instead of just finding eggs, we found a world full of wonderful traditions!

In Australia, they celebrate with barbecues and fun; in Greece, church services shine like Easter morning sun. Israel mixes culture with joy, and in Romania, families gather to enjoy.

Over in France, church bells ring, and in Brasil, people dance and sing. Spain feasts and prays, and in the Ethopia, Easter brings communal delight.

Germany, Norway, and across the sea, each place adds its flavor to the Easter glee. from lively celebrations to heartfelt prayers, the world comes together, showing that Easter love is everywhere.

So, whether you're in the snow or under the sun's bright light, Easter unites us all, making the world feel just right. And as we close this book with a cheer, let's celebrate Easter joy, year after year! Happy Easter, friends, in every land and nation—may your Easter be filled with pure jubilation!

HAPPY
EASTER

www.ingramcontent.com/pod-product-compliance
Lightning Source LLC
Chambersburg PA
CBHW081952160726
47999CB00008B/2606